Tales of Love and Lust

Palmwine Publishing

Palmwine Sounds

Copyright ©Palmwine Publishing Limited Nigeria

All rights reserved. No part of this publication may be reproduced, distributed, or transmitted in any form or by any means, including photocopying, recording, or other electronic or mechanical methods, without the prior written permission of the publisher, except in the case of brief quotations embodied in critical reviews and certain other non-commercial uses permitted by copyright law.

Author- Palmwine Sounds

ISBN (Paperback)- 978-1-917267-68-7

ISBN (E-Book)- 978-1-917267-69-4

Year Published- 2025

Published by Nubian Republic Ltd Uk on behalf of Palmwine Publishing Limited Nigeria

Email: info@palmwinepublishing.com

Address-Nigeria: 1A Jos Road Bukuru, Plateau State, Nigeria.

www.palmwinepublishing.com
www.raffiapress.com
www.nuciferaanalysis.com

Delilah

As my gaze was blessed with your presence.
I was yours, from my dreadlocks to toe nails.
The spell your projected my way,
Put me in a perfect gengetsu (illusion).

A face which I avoid glancing at,
Because you would see me blush.
Is it your pearly silky black skin,
Glistening like calm evening waters.
Or is it your perfect curves,
Such curvatures are extraordinary.
Maybe your calm confident voice,
Which can calm King Saul's demons.

Whatever the spell is,
Do not bother tempering.

My Heart

Tinko Tinko
My heartbeats
It is for love or lust
Or an equal mix of both.

Come let's dance around
And we would surely find out.

Shy

I may exude confidence
But in the game of love
Am a whimsical person

When I see you smile
From a distance
I begin to shiver

As I approach
Or you approach
My nerves tingle

On facing each other
Seen the dimples in your smile
The right words are projected

Maybe love
Is the comfort
I feel around you.

True North

My true north has changed on my compass.
It no longer points to places or things I once desired.
It now points towards your aura and being.
This may just be my simplistic sexual urges.
Or complex emotions I am trying to fathom.
Your body calls to me
And if you would let me,
I would submit to you.

What is Love?

I know lust
Fell to it snares

But what is love?
Come,
Let's find the definition.

Love and Lust

Feelings so close,
Yet very far apart.

Which is this?

One dances with the soul.
The other just touches the flesh.

Your Posterior

This may be lust after all.
She may be the fairest of them all.
Because when she blesses me,
By turning to her backside,
My heart always skips a bit.
The devil had to be involved in her creation.
Because I fall to my primal urges.

The Chase

The chase is a paramount to the love game.
But I would not chase forever,
If the feeling is not reciprocated.
I may love you, but won't lose myself.

So let me love you,
Or you can be,
Another obstacle,
In my quest for love.

The Kiss

Flowers, rainbows, unicorns,
And everything nice;
When we first met
You claimed you hated kisses
But when our lips first touch
I felt an echo in you resonating in me
The trumpets in the heavens,
Sounded, celebrating our love.

Chemistry

Our chemistry has intertwined.
You know my do's, I know your don'ts.
I know what makes you happy;
You know what makes me sad.
I am at peace when I am around you.
The shy girl I once knew is no more.
Even talking over my voice,
Paying no attention to what I say,
I remember all you say,
Even the ones you forgot you said.
I let you be the pilot,
Let me enjoy the ride.

Lovers Rocking

Young rasta me, is in love
The love songs now have meaning
Bed Jamming to Lee Perry
Loving to some Gregory Isaac
Sail across oceans, with Freddie McGregor
Lucky Dube seals the Romeo and Juliet tale.

Echoes at Midnight

At the stroke of midnight
Two lovers intertwined
One moaning in soprano
Other responding in tenor.

As the night ticked away
They switch their vocals
One to a softer contralto
Other responding in bass.

They called and responded
Toward each other's vocals
The night suddenly went quiet
As both climax in falsetto.

www.ingramcontent.com/pod-product-compliance
Lightning Source LLC
Chambersburg PA
CBHW060035180426
43196CB00045B/2693